SIGHT READING
& RHYTHM
EVERY DAY®

Helen Marlais with Kevin Olson

T H E
F·J·H
M U S I C
COMPANY
I N C.
Frank J. Hackinson

Production: Frank J. Hackinson
Production Coordinator: Philip Groeber
Cover: Terpstra Design, San Francisco
Text Design and Layout: Terpstra Design and Maritza Cosano Gomez
Engraving: Tempo Music Press, Inc.
Printer: Tempo Music Press, Inc.

ISBN-13: 978-1-56939-618-6

ABOUT THE AUTHORS

Dr. Marlais is one of the most prolific authors in the field of educational piano books and an exclusive writer for The FJH Music Company Inc. The critically acclaimed and award-winning piano series, *Succeeding at the Piano®* *A Method for Everyone, Succeeding with the Masters®, The Festival Collection®, In Recital®, Sight Reading and Rhythm Every Day®, Write, Play, and Hear Your Theory Every Day®,* and *The FJH Contemporary Keyboard Editions,* among others, included in *The FJH Pianist's Curriculum®* by Helen Marlais, are designed to guide students from the beginner through advanced levels. Dr. Marlais has given pedagogical workshops in virtually every state in the country and presents showcases for FJH at the national piano teachers' conventions. As well as being the Director of Keyboard Publications for The FJH Music Company, Dr. Marlais is also an Associate Professor of Music at Grand Valley State University in Grand Rapids, Michigan, where she teaches piano majors, directs the piano pedagogy program, and coordinates the young beginner piano program. She also maintains an active piano studio of beginner through high school age award-winning students. Dr. Marlais has given collaborative recitals throughout the United States and in Canada, Italy, England, France, Hungary, Turkey, Germany, Lithuania, Estonia, China and Australia, and has premiered many new works by contemporary composers from the United States, Canada, and Europe. She has performed with members of the Chicago, Pittsburgh, Minnesota, Grand Rapids, Des Moines, Cedar Rapids, and Beijing National Symphony Orchestras and has recorded on Gasparo, Centaur and Audite record labels with her husband, concert clarinetist Arthur Campbell. She has also recorded numerous educational piano CD's on Stargrass Records®. Dr. Marlais received her DM in piano performance and pedagogy from Northwestern University and her MFA in piano performance from Carnegie Mellon University. Visit: www.helenmarlais.com

Kevin Olson is an active pianist, composer, and member of the piano faculty at Utah State University, where he teaches piano literature, pedagogy, and accompanying courses. In addition to his collegiate teaching responsibilities, Kevin directs the Utah State Youth Conservatory, which provides weekly group and private piano instruction to more than 200 pre-college community students. The National Association of Schools of Music has recently recognized the Conservatory as a model for pre-college piano instruction programs. Before teaching at Utah State, he was on the faculty at Elmhurst College near Chicago and Humboldt State University in northern California.

A native of Utah, Kevin began composing at age five. When he was twelve, his composition, *An American Trainride,* received the Overall First Prize at the 1983 National PTA Convention at Albuquerque, New Mexico. Since then he has been a Composer in Residence at the National Conference on Piano Pedagogy, and has written music commissioned and performed by groups such as the American Piano Quartet, Chicago a cappella, the Rich Matteson Jazz Festival, and several piano teacher associations around the country. Kevin maintains a large piano studio, teaching students of a variety of ages and abilities. Many of the needs of his own piano students have inspired more than 100 books and solos published by The FJH Music Company Inc., which he joined as a writer in 1994.

FJH1541

HOW THE SERIES IS ORGANIZED

| All rhythmic activities | All sight-reading activities | All Rhythm Flash!, Pattern Flash! and Chord Flash! activities | Place a ✔ when you have been successful! |

Each unit of the series is divided into five separate days of enjoyable rhythmic and sight-reading activities. Students complete these short daily activities "Every Day" at home, by themselves. Every day the words, "Did It!" are found in a box for the student to check once they have completed both the rhythm and sight-reading activities.

The new concepts are identified in the upper right-hand corner of each unit. Once introduced, these concepts are continually reinforced through subsequent units.

On the lesson day, there are short rhythmic and sight-reading activities that will take only minutes for the teacher and student to do together. An enjoyable sight-reading duet wraps up each unit.

BOOKS 4A AND 4B

Rhythm:

Rhythmic activities in books 4A and 4B include the following:

- Students internalize the rhythms in many ways by clapping, tapping, stomping on the floor, pointing, and snapping their fingers.
- Triplet rhythms in simple time signatures are reinforced.
- Students say lyrics in rhythm.
- Students learn about *tenuto* markings.
- Students add bar lines and correct time signatures to excerpts and then count the examples out loud.
- Students are asked to clap rhythmic examples by memory—an excellent ear training and memory exercise.
- Students tap different rhythms in both hands.
- Students continue to drill the time signatures of $\frac{3}{4}$, $\frac{4}{4}$, and $\frac{6}{4}$.
- "Rhythm Flashes" are short rhythmic patterns that students look at briefly and then are asked to tap by memory. This skill helps them to think and prepare quickly.

Fingering:

Very little fingering is provided so that students learn to look ahead and think about patterns. Students are sometimes asked to decide their own fingering and write it directly in their score before starting to play.

Tips for Sight Reading:
- Decide the time and key signatures.
- Look for patterns in the music (intervals, phrases, rhythms).
- Sing or hum the piece in your mind.
- Plan the fingering.
- Make sure you count the rhythm at a steady tempo before starting.
- Plan the sound before you play.

Tips when playing:
- Sight read at a tempo that you can keep steady, without stopping.
- Keep your eyes on the music, and not on your hands.

Reading:

Students continue to identify melodic and harmonic intervals of major and minor 2nds, major and minor 3rds, and perfect 4ths and 5ths and begin 6th intervals and octaves in book 4A. Students learn major and minor 7th intervals in book 4B. Plagal and authentic chord progressions in major and minor and cross-hand arpeggios are reinforced. Students prepare for octave scales by playing pieces where the thumb slides under the third finger in order to extend past the usual five-finger patterns. One-octave scales begin in book 4A with C, G, D, and A major. Students are asked to focus on balancing simple melodies over simple accompaniments.

All major and minor white keys are reinforced as well as B flat major. Students are asked to transpose short pieces up or down to the nearest key as well as up or down a fifth interval. Students learn how to harmonize using chord symbols in book 4B. Students also read intervals from the high C and low C ledger lines.

Sight Reading activities include the following:

- "Pattern Flashes" and "Chord Flashes" are short patterns that students play or look at briefly and then are asked to play by memory, further helping to look ahead and think and prepare quickly.
- Students learn to "plan" for note and rhythmic accuracy, for correct articulations, and for a good sound.
- Students are asked to "hear" what the music is supposed to sound like before they start to play.
- Helpful suggestions guide students to think before they play and to not stop once they have started!
- Students are asked to sing or hum the melody of some of the excerpts, which encourages them to listen while maintaining a constant pulse and the forward motion of the musical line.
- Students circle intervals, patterns, and crossovers before playing.
- The metronome is used frequently.

FJH1541

TABLE OF CONTENTS

Unit 1

DAY ONE

New Concepts: sliding the thumb under the third finger; *tenuto* markings; reading intervals that include ledger lines

 Rhythm—Clap or tap the following rhythm with energy!

DID IT!

Place a ✔ when you have been successful!

 Rhythm—Clap the upper line, snap the middle line, and stomp the lower line of the example below.

DID IT!

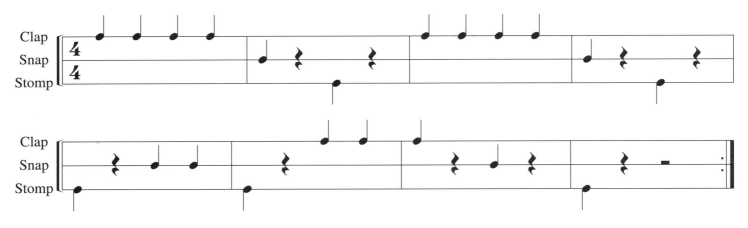

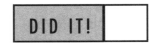 Sight reading—Circle the two places where the thumb slides under the third finger. Tap and count the example twice correctly before playing.

DID IT!

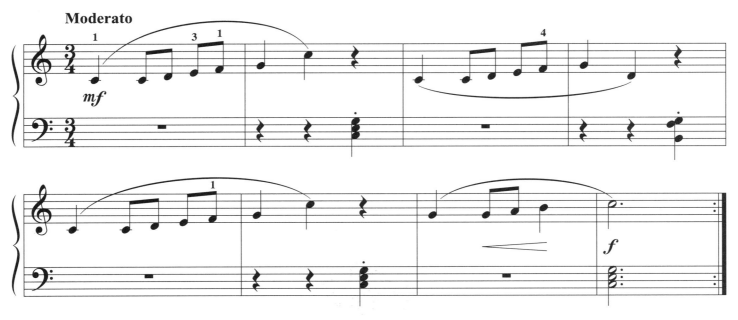

FJH1541

Rhythm—Tap and count out loud the following example, keeping it steady all the way through!

DID IT! ☐

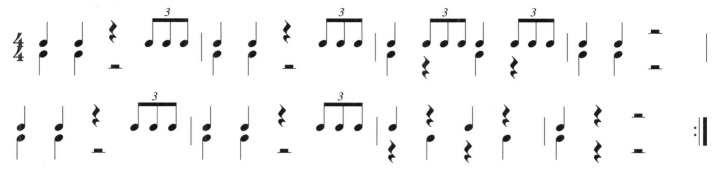

 Rhythm Flash!—Look at the first example for only a few moments and then look away from the book. Can you clap it from memory? Then try the same with the second example.

DID IT! ☐

 Sight reading—Is this example in C major or A minor? _____
Look through the entire piece and find the places where the R.H. thumb crosses under the third finger. Now play it all the way through without stopping!

Rhythm—Clap and count aloud with energy in your voice.

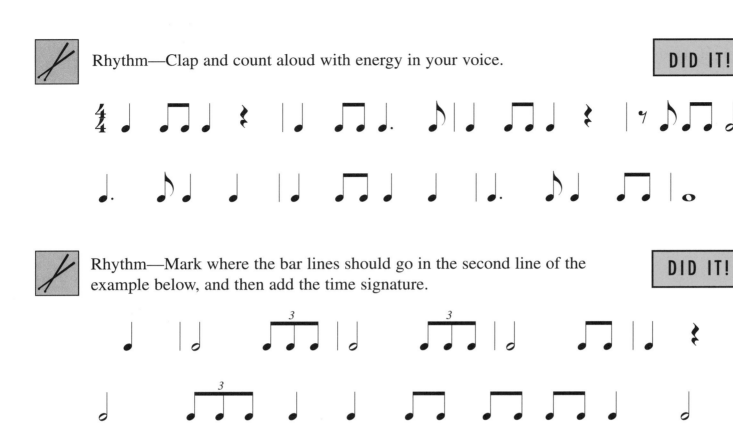

Rhythm—Mark where the bar lines should go in the second line of the example below, and then add the time signature.

Sight reading—Play all of the following C's on the keyboard. Circle the ledger line C's before you begin the piece. On the repeat, try to play this example without looking at your hands and just feeling the jumps!

hold the damper (right) pedal down throughout

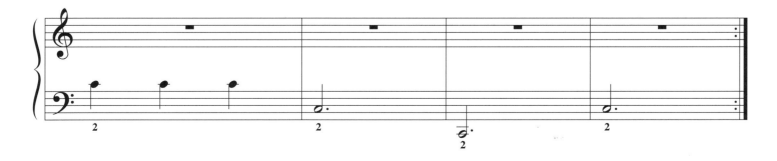

FJH1541

Rhythm—Tap the following exercise with the metronome set at ♩ = 80.

DID IT!

 Rhythm—Using the following rhythm, improvise a melody on the keyboard in the key of A minor.

DID IT!

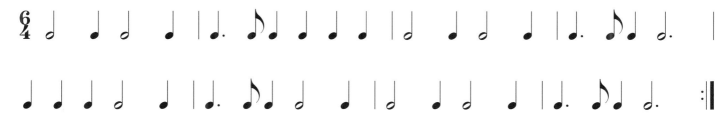

 Sight reading—Notice the *tenuto* signs in the piece below (̄ͅ). The *tenuto* mark tells us to give the note its full value as well as a slight emphasis. Circle all of the fifth intervals in the piece. Count while you play the piece on the top of the keys silently—can you "hear" the melody in your head?

DID IT!

DAY FIVE

Rhythm—Set a steady tempo first. When you see a note marked with an X, snap your fingers or tap on the wood of the piano. Clap the rest of the notes.

DID IT!

Rhythm—Point to each note as you say the lyrics in rhythm.

DID IT!

Have you ev - er no - ticed the led - ger line C notes a - bove and be - low the staves

look the same? They each have two led - ger lines!

Sight reading—Circle all of the C's in the piece below.

DID IT!

Andante

★ **LESSON DAY**

DID IT!

Your teacher will choose any rhythm or sight-reading example from this unit. Remember to take some time and prepare the example before you tap or play through it without stopping!

FJH1541

Ensemble Piece

DID IT! ☐

Tap and count the rhythm of the student part. Circle all of the perfect octave (P8) intervals before you begin. On which degree of the C major scale does the melody begin? _____ On which degree of the scale does the melody end? _____

Oh, Say Can You "C"?

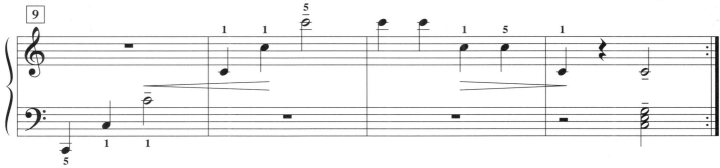

Teacher accompaniment (student plays one octave higher)

? After playing, ask yourself, "Did I play at a tempo that I can keep steady? Did I play with a relaxed arm and wrist?"

Unit 2

New Concepts: C major one-octave scales;
cross-hand arpeggios in the keys of C, G, D, and
B flat major. Review of I-V$_5^6$-I cadences and triplets

Rhythm—Circle all of the measures that have the same rhythmic pattern.
Then tap the upstem notes with your right hand and the downstem notes
with your left hand.

DID IT!

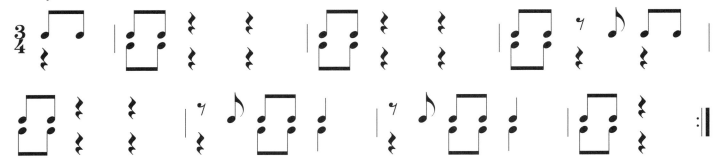

Rhythm Flash!—Look at the following examples for 20 seconds or less.
Close the book and try to clap each from memory!

DID IT!

Sight reading—Notice the one-octave scales in the example below.
Prepare the I and V$_5^6$ chords—How do they sound? What do they feel like?
Listen for a steady pulse as you play with confidence!

DID IT!

FJH1541

Rhythm—Add a note or rest to make sure each measure has the correct number of beats. Then tap with a steady beat.  DID IT!

 Rhythm—Clap the following example while you count. Follow the *crescendo* markings, too!  DID IT!

 Sight reading—Notice the cross-hand arpeggios in the piece below. Are the arpeggios ascending or descending? _____ With the metronome set at ♩ = 96, clap or tap the example and then play it at the same speed. If you make a mistake, keep going! DID IT!

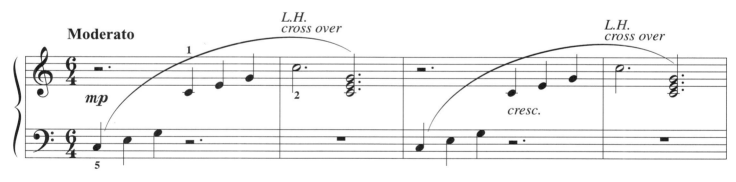

Transpose this piece up a fifth to the key of G major. _____

3
DAY THREE

 Rhythm—Decide the time signature and write it in at the beginning of the example. Then clap and count with confidence.

DID IT!

 Rhythm—Tap the following rhythmic example, keeping the beat as even as the ticking of a clock!

DID IT!

 Sight reading—Determine the key and notice the cross-hand arpeggios. Silently and steadily play the example on the top of the keys. When you think you can play the piece accurately, go ahead and play out loud!

DID IT!

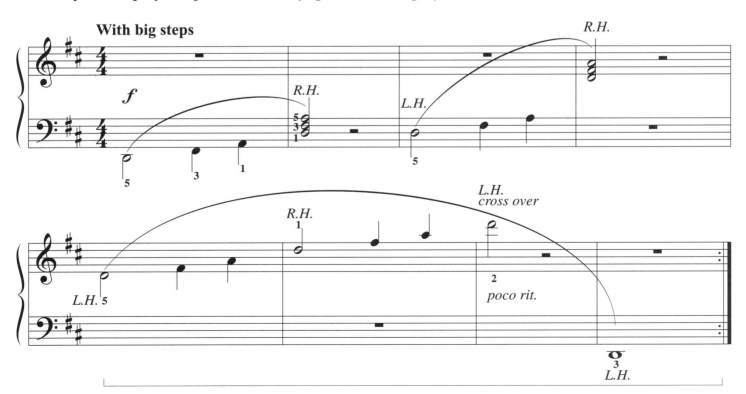

FJH1541

Rhythm—Point to each note as you say the lyrics in rhythm.

DID IT!

Rhythm—Tap and count the following exercise with the metronome set at ♩ = 72.

DID IT!

Sight reading—Notice the five-finger patterns from each of the C's.

DID IT!

Now try transposing the example above to two of the following keys: D major _____   F major _____

A major _____   B♭ major _____

Rhythm Flash!—Clap and count the first example below and then close the book. Can you clap and count it steadily from memory? Then try the same for the second example.

DID IT!

Rhythm—Clap the top line, snap the middle line, and stomp the third line.

DID IT!

Sight reading—What key is this piece in? _____ Count the rhythm of the example silently in your mind and then silently play it on the top of the keys. Plan the sound before you begin!

DID IT!

★ LESSON DAY

DID IT!

Your teacher will choose any rhythm example from this unit to tap. Remember to take some time and look at it before you start!

FJH1541

Ensemble Piece

Clap and count the rhythm of the melody below. Then play the beginning pitch of the melody. Can you hum or sing the entire melody? (Hint: if you get stuck, play the notes while you sing). Plan the blocked chords in the second line before beginning.

Hand Over Hand

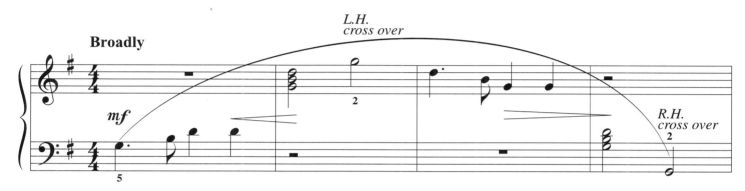

Teacher accompaniment (student plays one octave higher)

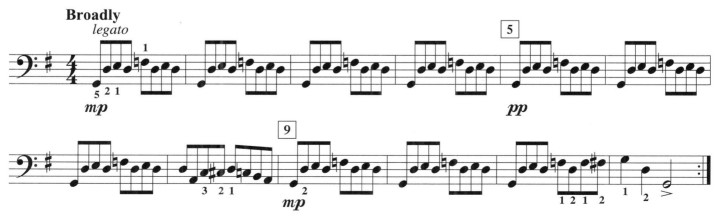

? After playing, ask yourself, "Did I consistently look ahead so that I could prepare well?"

Unit 3

New Concepts: G and D major
one-octave scales; interval of a sixth;
major and minor chords in various keys.
Review of I-V$_5^6$-I cadences

Rhythm—With the metronome set at ♩ = 72, clap and count with confidence!

DID IT!

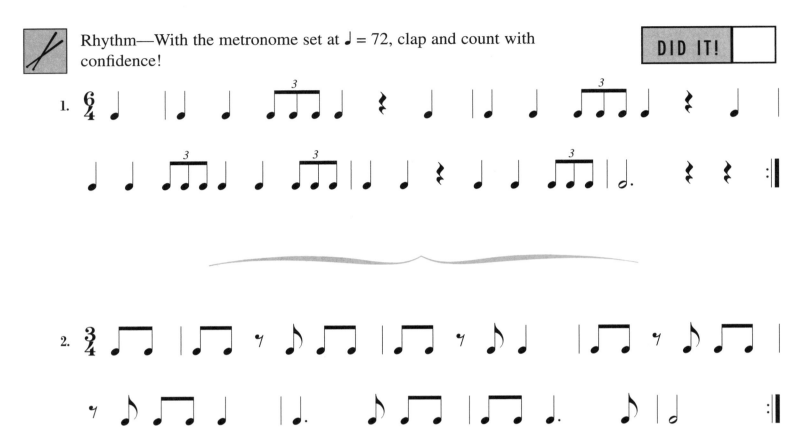

Sight reading—Circle the sixth intervals in the piece below, and then circle the only G major octave scale. Clap the rhythm slowly and evenly. Add the fingering in at the beginning of the piece and then play!

DID IT!

FJH1541

Rhythm—Add the correct time signature at the beginning of the example below, and then add bar lines to line 2. Then clap and count with confidence!

DID IT!

Pattern Flash!—How are the two phrases below different?
Play the first phrase and then close the book—try to play it from memory!
Then do the same with the second example.

DID IT!

Sight reading—With the metronome set at ♩ = 92, clap or tap the following example. Then play it at the same tempo. Can you repeat the process at ♩ = 104?

DID IT!

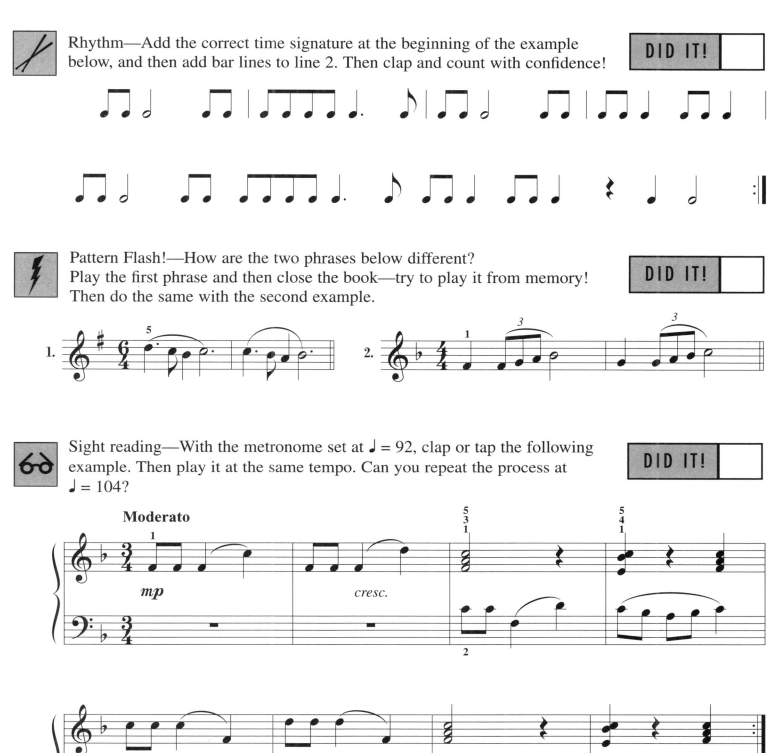

How would you rate your sight reading on a scale from 1–5? (5 being the highest) _____

Rhythm—Read the following lyrics in rhythm while you clap the beat or point to each note.

DID IT!

Can you say this three times fast: "We sure-ly shall see the sun shine soon.

We sure-ly shall see the sun shine soon. We sure-ly shall see the sun shine soon!"

Chord Flash!—Look at the following major and minor chords. Write the letter name of the chord as well as "M" for major or "m" for minor on the lines provided. Then play each chord, keeping a steady beat.

DID IT!

chord name: **CM**

Sight reading—Circle the two suspended fourth (sus4) chords below and then prepare them. Establish a pulse and play only the downbeats of the piece below. Play it once again, this time adding all of the other beats. Keep it steady!

DID IT!

Joyously

mf

mf

poco rit. 2nd time

Can you transpose this piece up a fifth interval to the key of D major? Yes or No _____

Rhythm—With your R.H., play the following rhythm pattern using the notes of a G major one-octave scale, being sure to end on the tonic (G) note. If you would like, you could add I and V^6_5 chords in the L.H. by ear.

DID IT!

G Major scale:

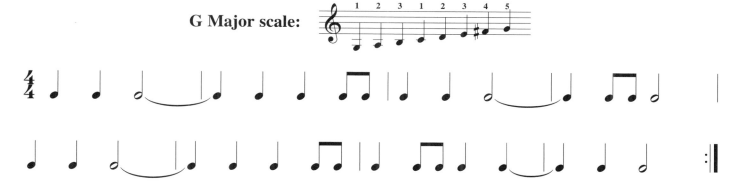

 Chord Flash!—Play the following example *adagio,* and then *allegro.* Can you play the example both ways from memory?

DID IT!

 Sight reading—Give yourself one minute to look at the following sight-reading piece. Think about how it is supposed to sound when you play it in regard to tempo, melody, rhythm, and articulations.

DID IT!

Can you transpose this piece to C major? Yes or No _____

DAY FIVE

Rhythm—Look at the entire example and count it in your mind.
Be sure to give each tied note its full value. How much of it can you clap
from memory? _____ measures.

DID IT!

Pattern Flash!—Circle the sixth intervals below. Then tap and count out loud.
Look at the first example carefully. Find the beginning note on the piano, close
the book, and try to play it from memory. On a scale from 1–5, how successful
were you? _____ Then try the same with the second example.

DID IT!

Sight reading—Circle the two sixth intervals in the B flat major melody
below. Tap and count evenly, and then when you play, always look ahead and
don't stop!

DID IT!

★ LESSON DAY

DID IT!

Your teacher will choose any rhythm or sight-reading example from this unit. Remember to take time
and think through it before you perform it without stopping!

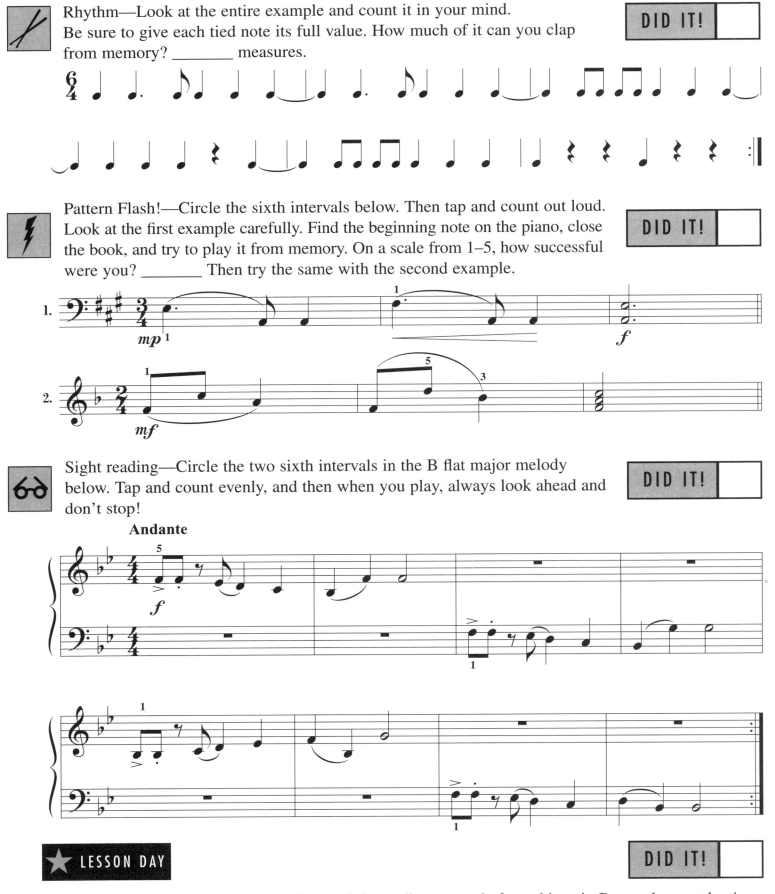

FJH1541

Ensemble Piece

Tap and count the rhythm of the student part. Plan the scales and the blocked intervals. Think about how the fourth, fifth, and sixth intervals feel differently. Plan the tempo and begin with your teacher.

Scaling to New Heights

Teacher accompaniment (student plays one octave higher)

After playing, ask yourself, "Did I keep going no matter what? Did I prepare well before playing?"

Unit 4

New Concepts: plagal (I-IV-I) cadences in the keys of C and G major; music terms *spiritoso* and *leggero*

Rhythm—Circle all of the measures that have the same rhythmic pattern. With the metronome set at ♩ = 72, clap and count with a steady rhythm!

DID IT! ☐

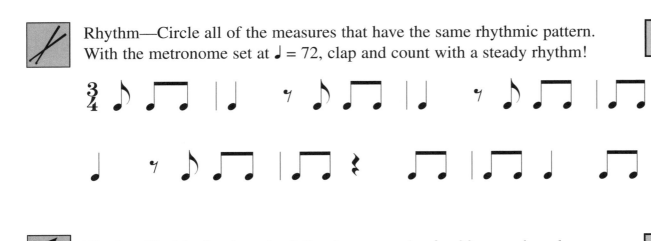

Rhythm Flash!—Look at the following examples for 20 seconds or less. Close the book and try to clap each from memory!

DID IT! ☐

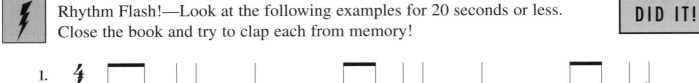

1.

2.

Sight reading—Draw a circle around all of the IV$_4^6$ chords before you play. How is line 2 different than line 1? _____
Keep a steady beat as you play the example, and don't stop!

DID IT! ☐

 Spiritoso (with spirit) ♩ = 120

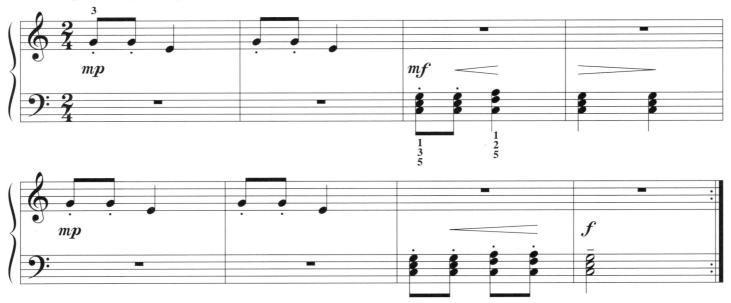

DAY TWO

Rhythm—Add a note or rest to make sure each measure has the correct number of beats. Then tap with a steady beat while counting out loud.

DID IT!

Rhythm—Clap the following example while you count. Wherever you see a notehead with an "X", stomp the floor.

DID IT!

Sight reading—Plan ahead: study the key and the rhythm. What interval has been circled throughout this piece? _____ Block (play together) this interval before sight reading the piece as written. Once you start, do not stop until the very end!

DID IT!

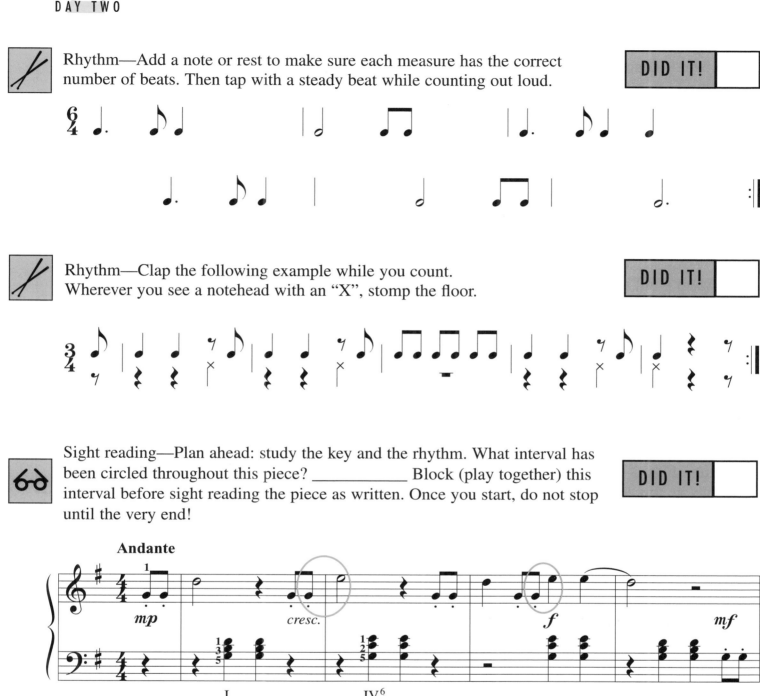

Can you transpose this piece up a fifth interval to the key of D major? _____
Can you transpose it to A major? _____ F major? _____

Rhythm—Clap and count first. Then point to each note while speaking the lyrics in rhythm.

DID IT!

Did you know that in Eng-land, they have some diff-'rent names for the notes? A

quar-ter note is called a crotch-et and an eighth note is called a qua-ver. Jol-ly good!

Rhythm—Fill in the missing bar lines, then clap with energy!

DID IT!

Pattern Flash!—Plan the first pattern flash below.
Can you play it without looking at the music?

DID IT!

1.

mf ff

Now play this pattern flash. In which measures do you see the subdominant (IV_4^6) chord? _____
and _____ .

2.

mf

If you were successful with this pattern flash, place a lightning bolt on the line! _____

DAY FOUR

 Rhythm—Play the following rhythm on the piano, using I and IV$^6_4$ chords in the key of G major.

 Chord Flash!—Look at the following major and minor chords. Write the letter name of the chord on the lines provided, as well as "M" for major or "m" for minor. You will use the same fingering for every chord. After playing the pattern, close the book and try to play it from memory!

Warmly

1
3
5

GM ___ ___ ___ ___ ___ ___ ___

 Sight reading—Tap and count the rhythm of the example below with a steady tempo. After you play it once in C major, transpose it up a fifth interval to G major.

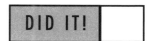

Leggero (light, nimble)

How would you rate your sight reading? _____ Excellent _____ Good _____ Fair _____ Poor

Rhythm—Clap and count aloud the following rhythm with energy at ♩ = 88. Then set the metronome at a quicker tempo, and clap it once more!

DID IT! ☐

Rhythm—Clap the top line, snap the middle line, and stomp the third line.

DID IT! ☐

Sight reading—Tap and count at ♩ = 66. Plan the dynamics and phrasing before starting. Add the fingering in at the beginning of the piece and wherever else you think you might need it. Then feel the pulse of the rhythm as you play!

DID IT! ☐

★ LESSON DAY

DID IT! ☐

Your teacher will choose any rhythm example from this unit to tap. Remember to take some time and prepare it before you start!

FJH1541

Ensemble Piece

Can you and your teacher sing or hum the melody of the piece below? Your teacher will give you one minute to look at the piece before you begin. Then play with confidence, always counting to keep a steady beat!

Barn Dance

Teacher accompaniment (student plays as written)

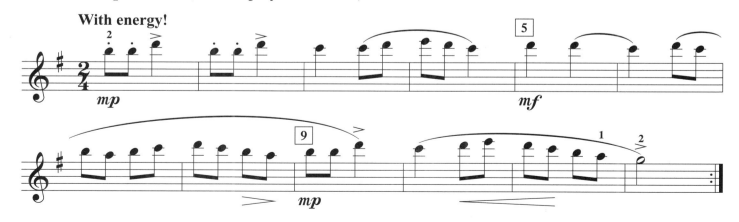

? After playing, ask yourself, "Did I play with energy, always looking ahead?"

Unit 5

New Concept: plagal cadences in the keys of F and D major. Review of D major one-octave scales and ledger line reading (high and low A's)

 Rhythm—At ♩ = 88, tap and count with energy!

DID IT!

 Pattern Flash!—How are the two phrases below similar? Play both phrases and then close the book—try to play them from memory!

DID IT!

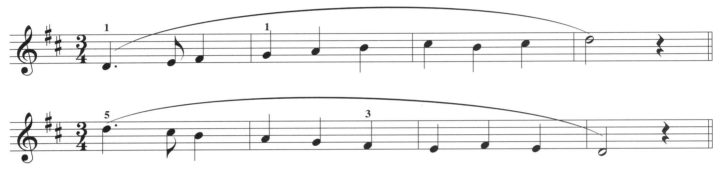

Sight reading—Plan the chords in your left hand. Then silently play the right-hand melody on the top of the keys. Where is the crossover? Circle it before you play. Tap and count the piece, and then play with confidence!

DID IT!

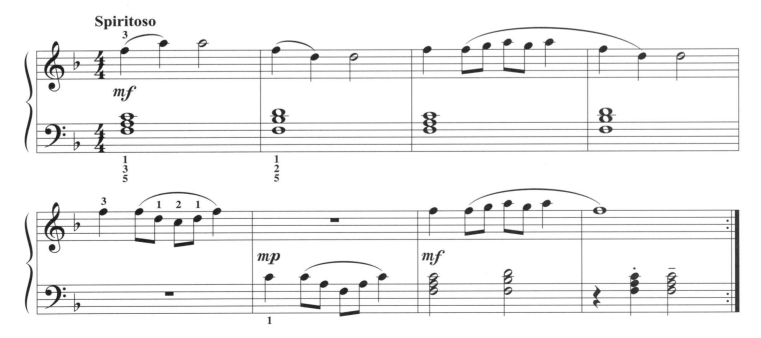

FJH1541

Rhythm—Carefully look at the following example. Then clap and count out loud steadily and accurately.

DID IT!

 Rhythm—Clap the following example and stomp your foot on every accented note.

DID IT!

 Sight reading—With the metronome set at ♩ = 92, clap or tap the sight-reading example below. Then play it at the same speed. Remember, counting while you play will help you keep a steady beat.

DID IT!

How would you rate your sight reading on a scale from 1–5? (5 being the highest) _____

Rhythm—Tap the example below, being sure to accent each accented note.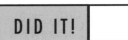

 Chord Flash!—How well can you find and play the following chords? Say the names of the chords as you play them. After you play them once with the R.H., try playing this example hands together, with your L.H. playing the same chords one octave below.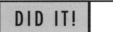

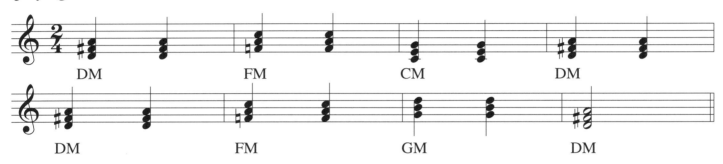

DM   FM   CM   DM

DM   FM   GM   DM

 Sight reading—Circle all of the broken IV_4^6 chords you can find in this example. The first one has been done for you. Where are the sixth intervals in the melody? Circle these as well. Tap and count before you begin and be sure you are confident of the piece before beginning.

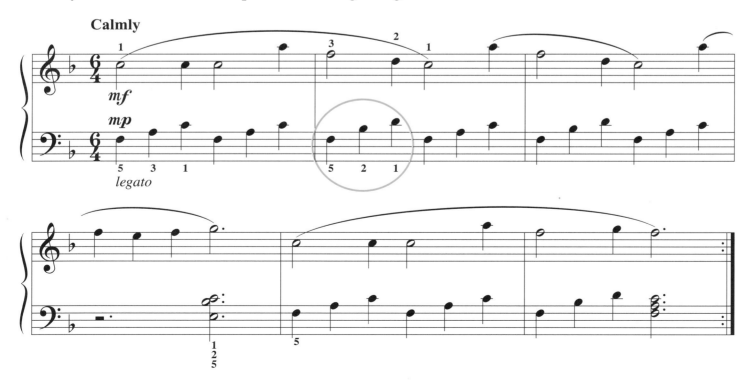

DAY FOUR

Rhythm—Speak the lyrics in rhythm as you point to each note.

DID IT!

There is one let-ter of the al-pha-bet that does-n't ap-pear in the names of an-y of the fif-ty U-nit-ed States. Can you name it?

(Answer at the bottom of the page)

Pattern Flash!—How fast can you find and play the following patterns? Sing them out loud or in your mind first!

DID IT!

Sight reading—Play the sight-reading example below at ♩ = 92, being sure that you count out loud and follow all of the musical markings.

DID IT!

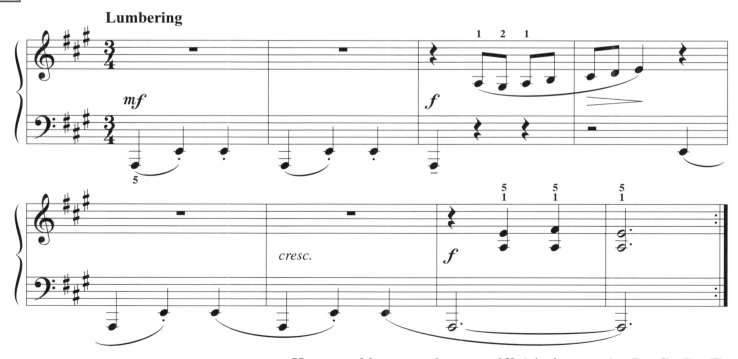

Lumbering

How would you grade yourself? (circle one: A B C D F)

(Answer to rhythm exercise: the letter Q.)

Rhythm—Add the correct time signature at the beginning of the example below, and then add bar lines to line 2. Then whisper the rests and tap the rhythm of the notes on your lap or on the fallboard.

DID IT!

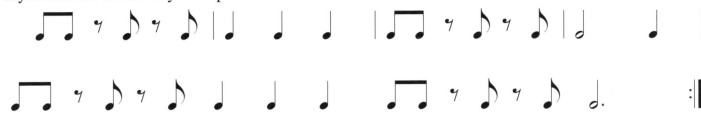

 Chord Flash!—Look at the following six chords for 30 seconds or less. Can you play them perfectly while you add the pedal?

DID IT!

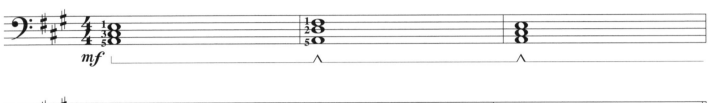

 Sight reading—Focus on the example below. How are measures 1–4 similar to measures 5–8? After you have tapped the rhythm of the entire piece, sight read it at ♩ = 84!

DID IT!

⭐ LESSON DAY

DID IT!

Your teacher will choose any sight-reading example from this unit. Remember to take some time and look at the music before you play through it without stopping!

FJH1541

Ensemble Piece

Tap the rhythm of the student part at ♩ = 72. Once you have tapped it correctly once, tap it three more times correctly. Scan the piece for the key and for patterns. Play it once without your teacher, adding the pedal. When your teacher joins you, (s)he can pedal for both of you!

A Sunday Morning Hymn

Teacher accompaniment (student plays one octave higher)

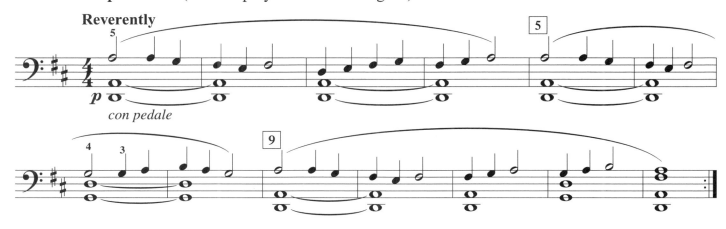

? After playing, ask yourself, "Did I take time to count each note for its full value?"

Unit 6

DAY ONE

New Concept: playing pieces with
I-IV_4^6-V_5^6-I chords in the keys of
C, G, D, and F major. Review of ledger line reading

Rhythm—Tap the following rhythmic example. Count out loud with energy in your voice!

DID IT!

Rhythm—Add the correct time signature at the beginning of the example below, and then add bar lines to line 2. Then clap and count out loud steadily.

DID IT!

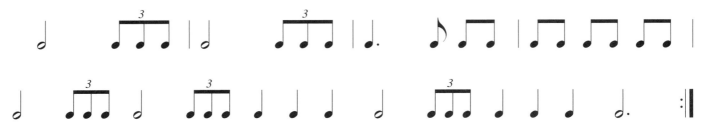

Sight reading—Clap and count the piece below at ♩ = 100. Be sure that your rhythm is steady and accurate before you play it, and that you have planned the patterns. The second time through you can add the dynamics.

DID IT!

36

FJH1541

Rhythm—Clap the following example while counting aloud. Knock on the wood of the piano wherever you see an "X" on a notehead.

DID IT!

Rhythm Flash!—How are the two phrases below different? _____
Play both phrases and then try to play them from memory!

DID IT!

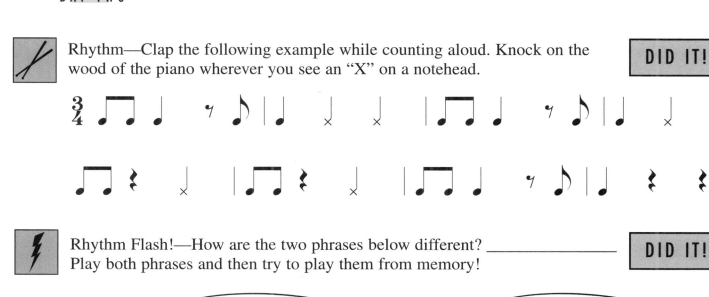

Sight reading—Scan the sight-reading piece below. Think of what the melodic fifths and sixths should sound like. Tap and count steadily before playing at ♩ = 76. Once you start, do not stop until the very end!

DID IT!

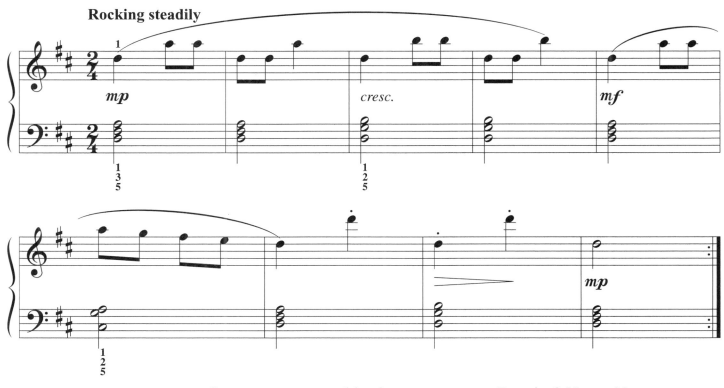

Can you transpose this piece up a step to E major? Yes or No _____

Rhythm—Tap the upper line, snap the middle line, and stomp the lower line of the example below.

DID IT!

Pattern Flash!—How fast can you find and play these patterns? Sing them out loud or in your mind first! Be sure to plan the L.H. chords carefully.

DID IT!

Sight reading—Circle the V^6_5 chord before you play, and then circle the measures that are exactly the same. Play the opening pitch in the right hand. Can you "hear" the entire melody in your mind before you play?

DID IT!

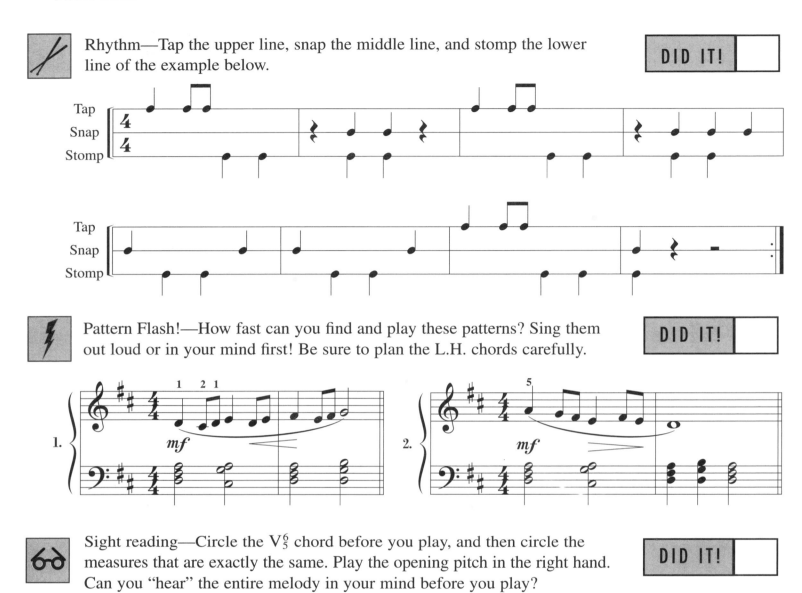

Spiritoso

4
DAY FOUR

Rhythm—Say the following lyrics in rhythm at ♩ = 92.
Try it once at this speed, then twice more quickly!

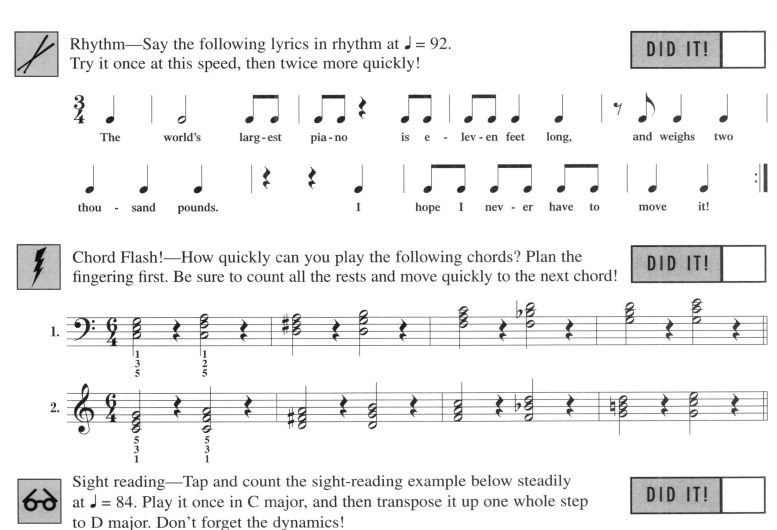

Chord Flash!—How quickly can you play the following chords? Plan the fingering first. Be sure to count all the rests and move quickly to the next chord!

Sight reading—Tap and count the sight-reading example below steadily at ♩ = 84. Play it once in C major, and then transpose it up one whole step to D major. Don't forget the dynamics!

How would you rate your sight reading on a scale from 1–10? _____

DAY FIVE

Rhythm—Look at the entire example and count it in your mind. Draw lines connecting measures that are exactly the same. How much of it can you clap from memory? _____ measures.

DID IT!

Pattern Flash!—Look at the first example below. Notice the sequence (pattern is the same but moves up every measure). After playing it, can you close the book and play it again by memory? Then follow the same steps with the second example.

DID IT!

Sight reading—Notice the 4th, 5th, and 6th intervals. Plan these carefully. When playing the example, as soon as you play a note, look ahead to the next one, always counting out loud.

DID IT!

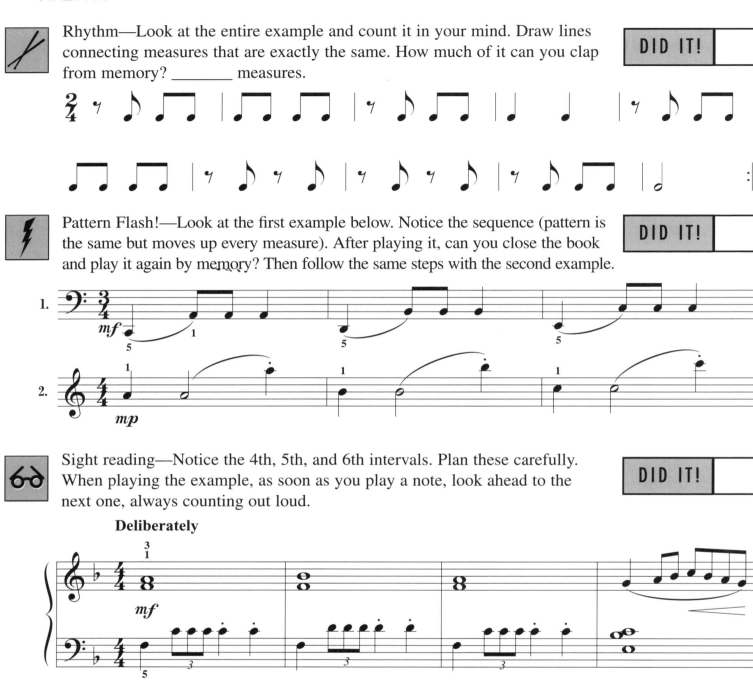

★ LESSON DAY

DID IT!

Your teacher will choose any rhythm or sight-reading example from this unit to sight read. Remember to take some time and look at the example before you sight read it without stopping!

FJH1541

Ensemble Piece

Count the student part below at ♩ = 84, being sure to count aloud. Plan the I and IV$^6_4$ chords.
When you play with your teacher, concentrate on playing it musically.

Jumping in Piles of Leaves

Teacher accompaniment (student plays LH one octave higher)

? After playing, ask yourself, "Did I always look
ahead to prepare for what was coming next?"

Unit 7

New Concepts: playing pieces with
I-IV$_4^6$-V$_5^6$-I chords in the keys of A and
E major; A major one-octave scales; music
term *allegretto*. Review of sequences

 Rhythm—Tap and count the following example with energy and without stopping, always looking ahead! Try it first at ♩ = 84, and then increase the tempo to ♩ = 92.

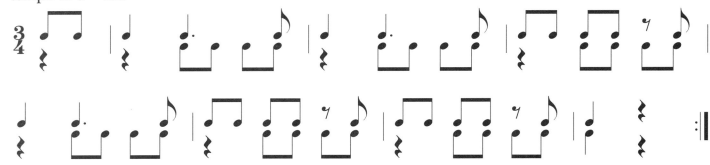

 Chord Flash!—How well can you play the following chords? Be sure to count carefully and move quickly to the next chord! Did you play each chord with the correct fingering? You can add pedal if you like.

 Sight reading—Draw a circle around each R.H. phrase that is a sequence of measure 1. The first one has been done for you. Where is the place where the second finger crosses over the thumb? measure _____
Listen for a steady pulse as you play slowly with confidence!

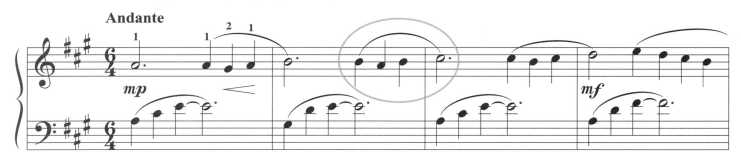

FJH1541

Rhythm—Clap the upper line, snap the middle line, and stomp the lower line of the example below. Be sure to accent the notes that need to be accented! How easy is this example for you? (Circle one: Easy   Not Easy)

DID IT!

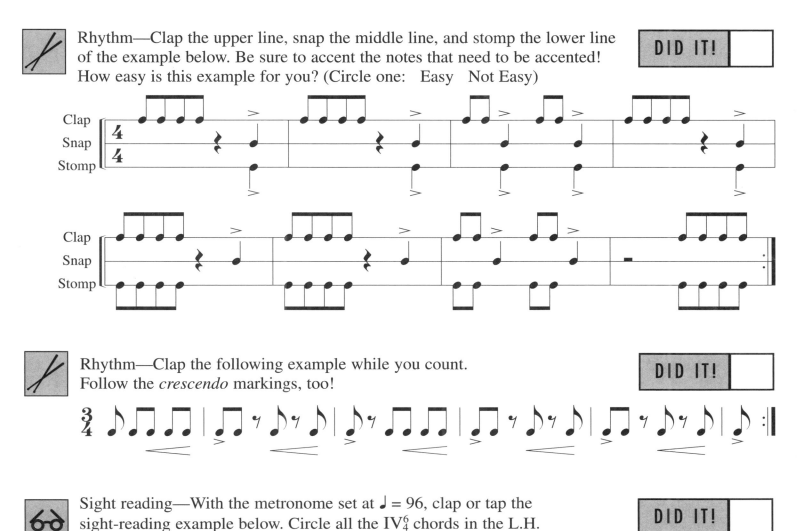

Rhythm—Clap the following example while you count. Follow the *crescendo* markings, too!

DID IT!

Sight reading—With the metronome set at ♩ = 96, clap or tap the sight-reading example below. Circle all the IV^6_4 chords in the L.H. Then play it at the same speed (tempo). If you make a mistake, keep going!

DID IT!

Allegretto (a little slower than allegro)

Can you find and circle the sequence in the melody in line 2?

Rhythm—Tap both lines, counting out loud.

DID IT! ☐

Pattern Flash!—Circle all of the A notes. Count and play steadily, always planning the next move. Play it one more time, this time adding the pedal.

DID IT! ☐

Not too quickly!

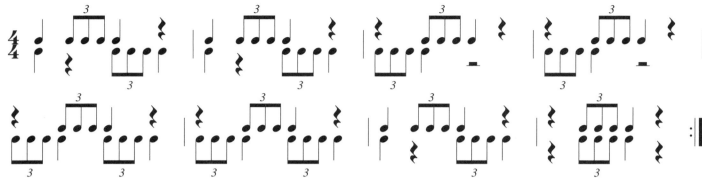

Sight reading—Play this example silently on the top of the keys first, without making a sound. Then play it out loud at the same tempo. If you make a mistake, keep going!

DID IT! ☐

Allegretto

FJH1541

Rhythm—Point to each note as you say the lyrics in rhythm.

DID IT! ☐

Here is a lit-tle joke a-bout a key we are learn-ing in this u-nit:

Which of the keys was an of-fic-er in the ar-my? A ma-jor!

 Rhythm Flash!—Look at the following pattern for 20 seconds or less. Close the book and try to tap the first 3 measures from memory!

DID IT! ☐

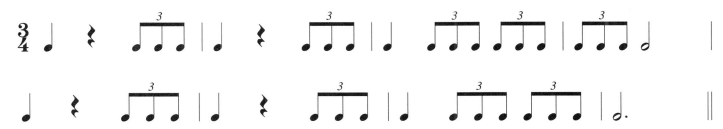

 Sight reading—Determine the key and find all of the perfect fourth intervals by marking them. The first one has been done for you. Circle the only place where the thumb slides under the third finger. Silently and steadily play the example on the top of the keys before beginning at ♩ = 63.

DID IT! ☐

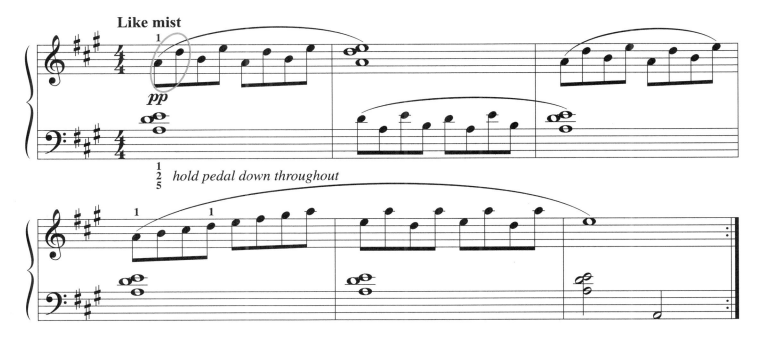

DAY FIVE

 Rhythm—Add the correct time signature at the beginning of the example below, and then add bar lines to line 2. Then clap and count steadily!

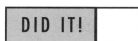 DID IT!

 Flash Pattern!—Look at the first phrase. Notice how this phrase is repeated, in sequence for the rest of the piece. Draw an arrow over the last measure (as the others have been done for you) indicating whether the sequence is ascending or descending. Play and count evenly.

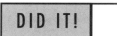 DID IT!

Sight reading—Notice the key signature, then tap and count out loud the sight-reading example below at ♩ = 92. When you play it, make sure that you bring out the melody over the accompaniment.

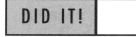 DID IT!

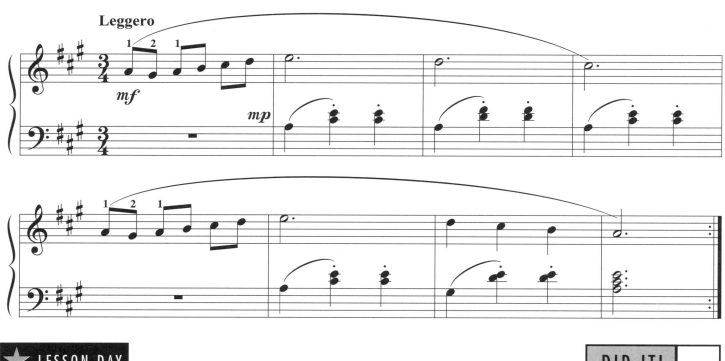

 LESSON DAY

DID IT!

Your teacher will choose any rhythm or sight-reading example from this unit to sight read. Remember to take some time and look at the example before you sight read it without stopping!

FJH1541

Ensemble Piece

Clap and count the rhythm of the melody below. Then play the beginning pitch of the melody.
Can you hum or sing the entire melody? (Hint: if you get stuck, play the notes while you sing).

The Bells of St. Mary's

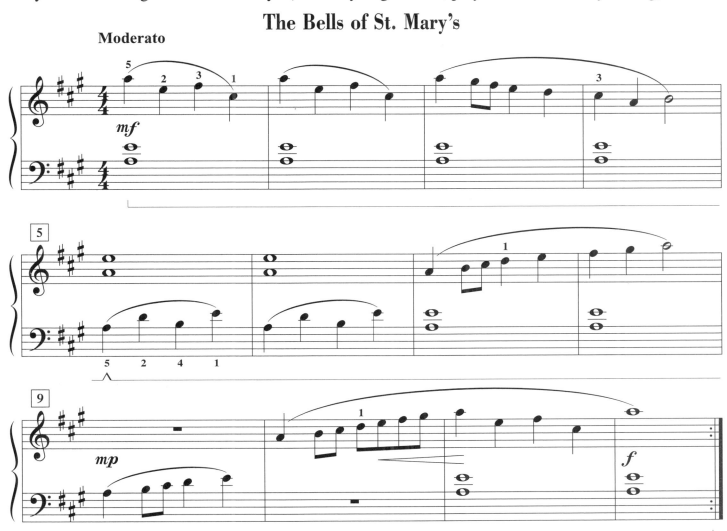

Teacher accompaniment (student plays as written)

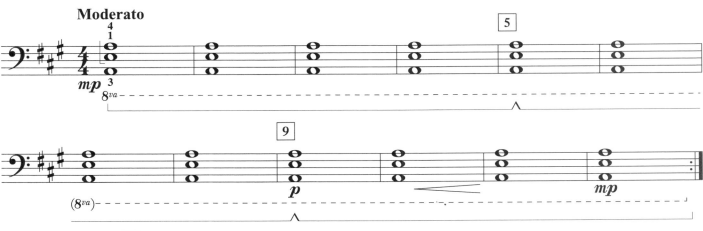

? After playing, ask yourself, "Did the duet sound like the chiming of bells? Did I keep going while counting, no matter what happened?"

Unit 8

 New Concept: playing pieces with
I-IV$_4^6$-V$_5^6$-I chords in the key of B flat major

 Rhythm—Clap or tap the following rhythm, accenting the downbeats as you count along!

 Rhythm Flash!—Tap the first example and then try to do it from memory. Then try the same with the second example.

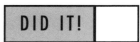

 Sight reading—Tap and count before playing. Prepare the right-hand chords silently before you play the piece hands together. Set a steady tempo and count while you play.

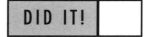

Lumbering along

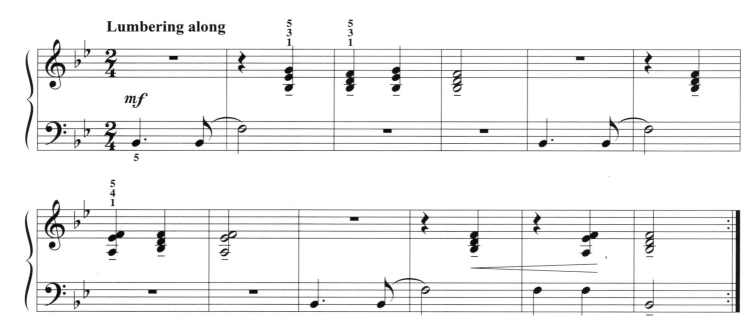

Rhythm—Add bar lines to the following rhythm. Then tap or snap your fingers, counting aloud.

 Rhythm—With the metronome set at ♩ = 92, clap the following rhythm and count aloud, making a *crescendo* to each downbeat.

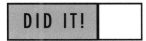

 Sight reading—Plan ahead: study the rhythm and the key of the following sight-reading example. Do you see any perfect fifths, crossovers, or crossunders? Which phrases are *exactly* the same? Practice the example silently on the top of the keys before playing.

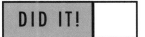

Can you transpose this to the key of F major? If so, place a smiley face on the line: _____

DAY THREE

Rhythm—Clap the upper line, snap the middle line, and stomp the lower line of the example below.

DID IT!

Pattern Flash!—Tap the following pattern at ♩ = 92 and then look at it for 20 seconds or less. How would you grade your sight reading?
A   B   C   D   F   (circle one)

DID IT!

Pattern Flash!—How well can you play these patterns? Decide the key and the tempo before you play them steadily and musically. Can you play each one without looking at the book?

DID IT!

FJH1541

Rhythm—At ♪ = 92, tap the upstem notes with your right hand and the downstem notes with your left hand.

DID IT!

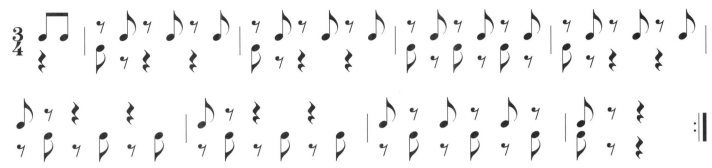

 Chord Flash!—Label each of the I, IV$_4^6$, and V$_5^6$ chords in the example below, then add the fingering. When you think you are ready, play while counting out loud and don't stop!

DID IT!

 Sight reading—Tap and count the sight-reading example below. Think about the key, time signature, and articulations. Play it through at a *forte* dynamic and concentrate on accuracy. When you repeat it, add all the dynamics and think about the musical shape of each phrase.

DID IT!

How would you rate your sight reading? _____ Excellent   _____ Good   _____ Fair   _____ Poor

Rhythm—Clap and count without stopping. Then point to each note as you say the lyrics in rhythm.

DID IT!

Is mid-dle C real-ly the mid-dle note on a pi-ano?

Count for your-self and see which note is half-way up to eight-y-eight!

(Answer at the bottom of the page)

Rhythm—Using the notes of a B flat major scale, improvise a melody using the following rhythm. If you would like to add I, IV$_4^6$, and V$_5^6$ chords in the L.H., try it!

DID IT!

Sight reading—Set the metronome at ♩= 63 and tap and count. Prepare the hand jumps at the end before you play. Do you know what the melody sounds like without playing it? (Give yourself the opening pitch and sing or hum it to make sure!)

DID IT!

Adagio

⭐ LESSON DAY

DID IT!

Your teacher will choose any rhythm example from this unit to tap. Remember to take some time and prepare the example before you tap it without stopping!

(Answer: The middle of the piano is between the E and F above middle C.)

FJH1541

Ensemble Piece

DID IT! [ ]

Prepare the piece in the following way: What is the key? _____ Look at the time signature and the patterns. Circle all the phrases that are the same. Take two minutes to look at the piece and think about how it should sound. Then play without stopping, always looking ahead!

When Sight Reading, Be Sharp or B♭!

Teacher accompaniment (student plays as written)

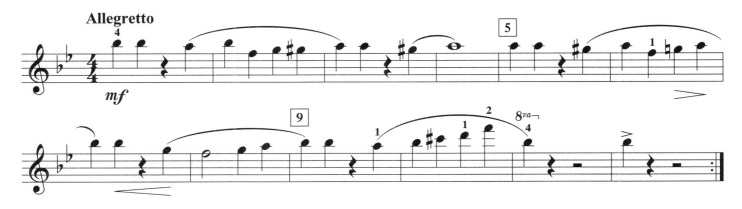

? After playing, ask yourself, "Did I play evenly and confidently? Did I count each rest?"

Unit 9

New Concept: playing pieces with
i-iv$_4^6$-V$_5^6$-i in the keys of A and D minor

Rhythm—With the metronome set at ♩ = 72, clap and count with energy!

DID IT!

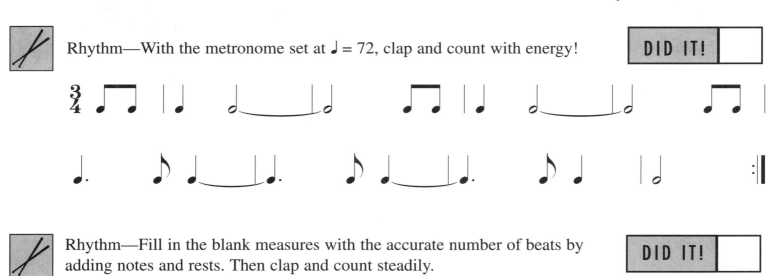

Rhythm—Fill in the blank measures with the accurate number of beats by adding notes and rests. Then clap and count steadily.

DID IT!

Sight reading—Is this piece in the key of A or D minor? _____ Circle the V$_5^6$ chords before you play and then circle the measures that are exactly the same. Play the opening five pitches in the right hand. Can you hear the entire melody in your mind before you play?

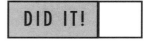

DID IT!

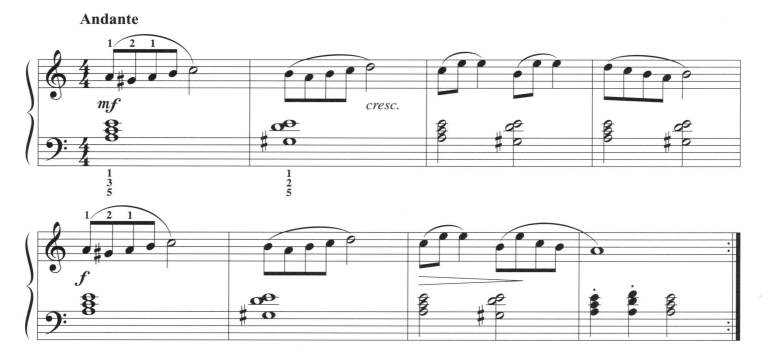

DAY TWO

Rhythm Flash!—Look at the first example for only a few moments and then look away from the book. Can you clap it from memory? Then try the same with the next pattern.

DID IT!

1.

2.

Pattern Flash!—Circle all of the A's. Count the pattern in your mind and then play while counting. Counting while you play will help you to keep a steady beat.

DID IT!

After you have sight read it in A minor, can you transpose it to D minor? _____

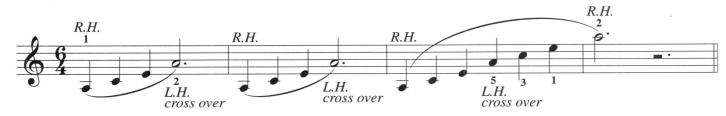

Sight reading—Play the sight-reading example at ♩ = 84. Then increase your tempo and focus on all of the articulation and dynamic markings.

DID IT!

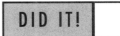 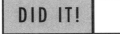

FJH1541

55

3
DAY THREE

Rhythm—Clap the upper line and stomp the lower line of the example below.

DID IT!

Chord Flash!—Look at the chords below. Can you memorize the chords and remember where they are played on the keyboard? When you are confident that you know, close the book and play the four phrases!

DID IT!

Pattern Flash!—How well can you find and play these patterns? Give yourself 20 seconds to plan each one. Sing them out loud or in your mind first!

DID IT!

56

FJH1541

Rhythm—Add the correct time signature at the beginning of the example below, and then add bar lines to line 2. Then clap and count with confidence!

DID IT!

Pattern Flash!—How fast can you find these patterns? Sing them out loud or in your mind first! As you prepare these examples, decide what makes each measure different.

DID IT!

Sight reading—Circle all of the D notes. What intervals are played from these D's?

DID IT!

How would you grade your performance? (circle one: A   B   C   D   F)

5

Rhythm—Read the following lyrics in rhythm while you clap the beat or point to each note.

DID IT!

Did you know that stu-dents who take   mu-sic les-sons   score   high-er than their peers   on

stan-dard-ized tests in math, sci-ence,   and   lan-guage arts?   All this prac-tic-ing is   mak-ing you   smart!

Chord Flash!—Play the following chordal pattern. How are measures 3–4 similar to measures 1–2? Then close the book and try to play it from memory!

DID IT!

♩ = m.m. 104

mf

Sight reading—Silently touch the chords before you play. Circle the places where the second finger crosses over the thumb. Giving yourself the opening pitch, can you hum the melody before you play?

DID IT!

Spiritoso

mp

cresc.

mf

f

⭐ **LESSON DAY**

DID IT!

Your teacher will choose any rhythm or sight-reading example from this unit to sight read. Remember to take some time and prepare the example before you start!

Ensemble Piece

DID IT!

Tap the rhythm of the student part at ♩ = 84. Once you have tapped it correctly once, tap it one more time correctly. Scan the piece for the key and for patterns.

Safari Sounds

Teacher accompaniment (student plays as written)

Exotically

? After playing, ask yourself, "Did I follow the dynamics? Did I count evenly? Did the duet sound like the title?"

Unit 10
Sight Reading and Rhythm Review

Rhythm—Tap and count out loud the following rhythm examples with the metronome, ♩ = 84.

DID IT!

Add the correct time signatures at the beginning of the examples below, and then add bar lines to line 2 of each example. Then clap and count out loud steadily.

DID IT!

Tap the upstem notes with your right hand and the downstem notes with your left hand.

DID IT!

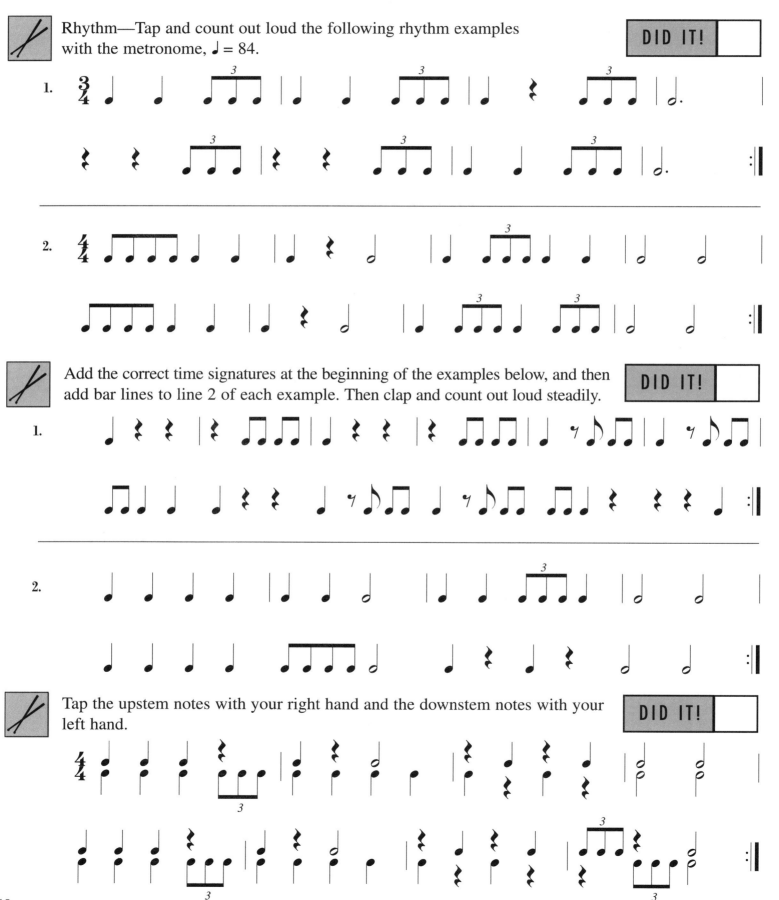

FJH1541

Write the key of each example in the space provided. Circle the IV$_4^6$ chords and plan the sound before you begin. Then tap and count at $\quarternote = 92$.

Key of _____

Can you transpose this example to the key of D major? _____

Key of _____

Can you transpose this example to the key of A major? _____

Key of _____

Can you transpose this example to the key of G major? _____

Plan the following cross-hand arpeggio, being sure to prepare the last chord as well. Plan the tempo and then play.

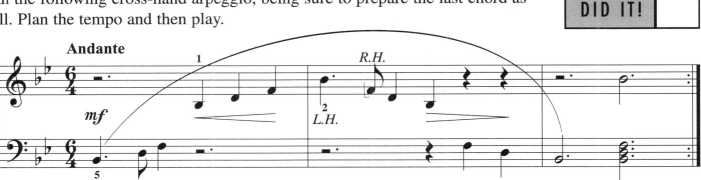

Which of the following keys can you transpose this example to?   C major _____   G major _____

D major _____   A major _____   E major _____   F major _____

Rhythm—Say the following lyrics in rhythm. Try it once slowly, then once as quickly as you can! Always speak steadily!

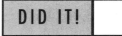 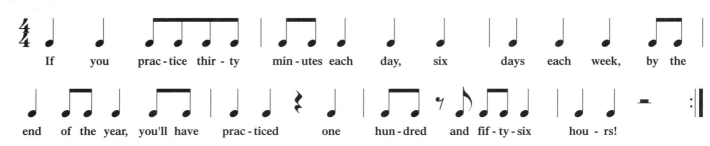

Chord Flash!—How well can you play the following I and IV$^6_4$ chords? Plan the fingering. Use the rests to look ahead and move quickly to the next measure.

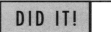

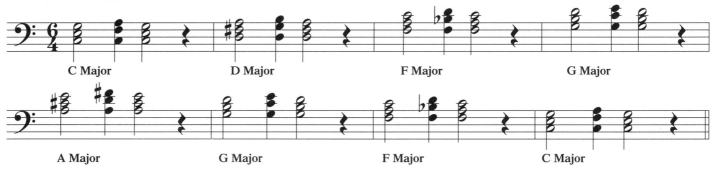

Sight reading—Tap and count the example below steadily. Practice the G major scale once with each hand before you begin this example, and then plan the chords. Don't forget to cross the thumb under the third finger!

FJH1541

Ensemble Piece

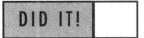

What key is this piece in? _____ What two chords do you play in the L.H.? _____
Tap the rhythm of this piece first, counting aloud with the metronome at ♩ = 92. When you play with
your teacher, concentrate on keeping the tempo steady and following all of the dynamic markings.

Shadow Dance

Teacher accompaniment (student plays one octave higher)

After playing, ask yourself, "Did the duet have the
sound and the feel of a dance?"

Additional Sight Reading Exercises

Unit 1: Find the crossovers and crossunders. Plan these before playing

Unit 2: Plan the scale fingering as well as the rhythm.

FJH1541

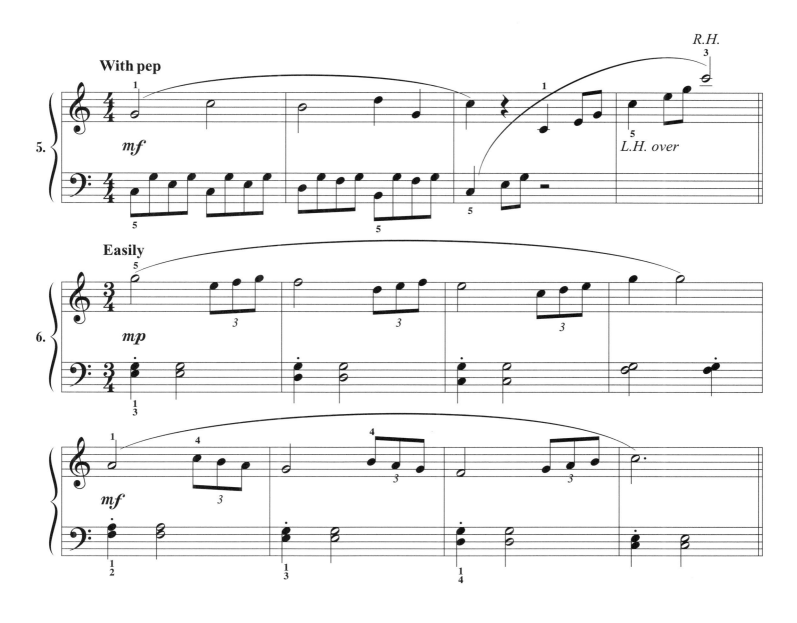

Unit 3: Find the intervals of a sixth. Play them. Then plan the rhythm.

Unit 4: Plan the plagal (I - IV - I) cadence.

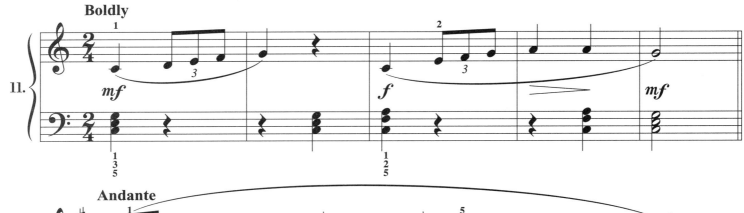

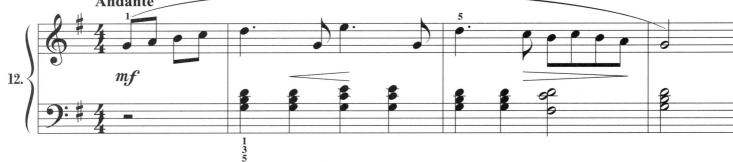

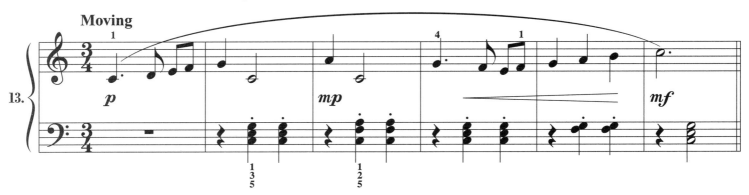

 FJH1541

Unit 5: Plan the I and IV$_4^6$ chords before playing.

Unit 6: Tap the rhythm, hands together, before playing at a steady tempo.

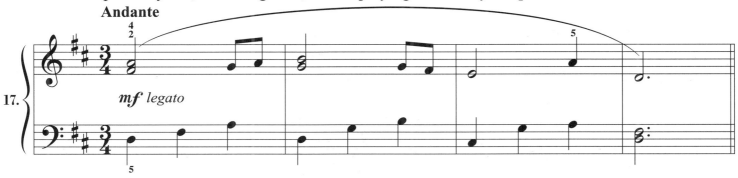

Unit 7: Play the exercises silently on the top of the keys before playing aloud.

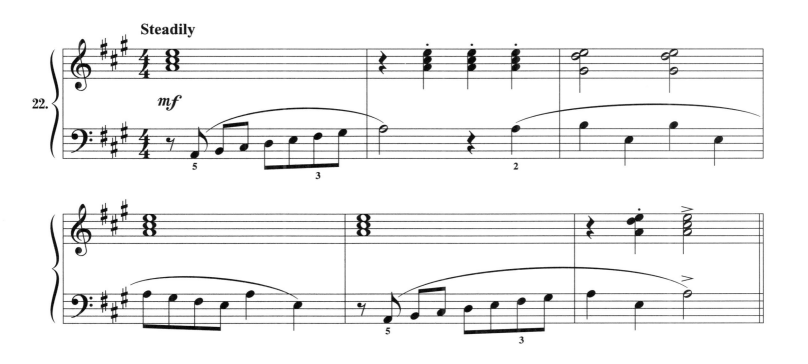

Unit 8: As you play, keep your eyes on the music and not on your hands.

Unit 9: Keep going, no matter what. Count while you play.

70

Unit 10: Before playing, tap the rhythm, hands together.

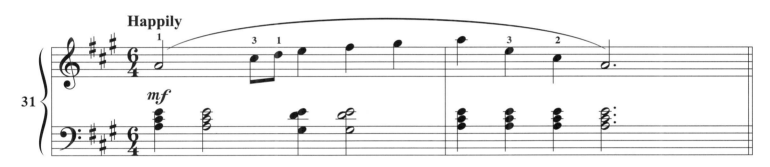

Certificate of Achievement

_____

has successfully completed

SIGHT READING & RHYTHM EVERY DAY®

BOOK 4A

of The FJH Pianist's Curriculum®

You are now ready for **Book 4B**

_____
Date

_____
Teacher's Signature

Selections from Harry Potter and the Goblet of Fire™

Instrumental Solos

M000107821

Project Manager: Carol Cuellar
Book Art Design: Ernesto Ebanks
Arranged by Bill Galliford, Ethan Neuburg and Tod Edmondson
Orchestral Sequencing by Francesco Marchetti
Recorded and Mixed by Pino Santamaria and Claudio Trippa
Clarinet, Alto Sax, Tenor Sax, Flute by Ferruccio Corsi
Trumpet by Mirko Rinaldi
Trombone by Massimo Pironi
French Horn by Rino Franco Pecorelli
Violin by Antonio Marchetti
Viola by Mara Coco
Cello by Luca Pincini

Music by Patrick Doyle
Except for HEDWIG'S THEME by John Williams

DEATH OF CEDRIC

By PATRICK DOYLE

FOXTROT FLEUR

By PATRICK DOYLE

HARRY IN WINTER

By PATRICK DOYLE

25406

POTTER WALTZ

By PATRICK DOYLE

THE QUIDDITCH WORLD CUP
(The Irish)

By PATRICK DOYLE

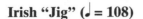

Irish "Jig" (♩ = 108)

The Quidditch World Cup - 2 - 1
25406

* An optional, more challenging figure has been provided in cue notes.

HOGWARTS' MARCH

By PATRICK DOYLE

Hogwarts' March - 2 - 1
25406

Hogwarts' March - 2 - 2
25406

NEVILLE'S WALTZ

By PATRICK DOYLE

Neville's Waltz - 2 - 1
25406

HOGWARTS' HYMN

By PATRICK DOYLE

Noble, with expression (♩ = 69)

HEDWIG'S THEME

By JOHN WILLIAMS

Misterioso

25406

© 2001 WARNER-BARHAM MUSIC, LLC
All Rights Administered by WARNER-TAMERLANE PUBLISHING CORP.
All Rights Reserved

PARTS OF AN ALTO SAXOPHONE AND FINGERING CHART

• When there are two fingerings given for a note, use the first one unless the alternate fingering is suggested.

• When two enharmonic notes are given together (F♯ and B♭ for example,) they sound the same pitch and are played the same way.

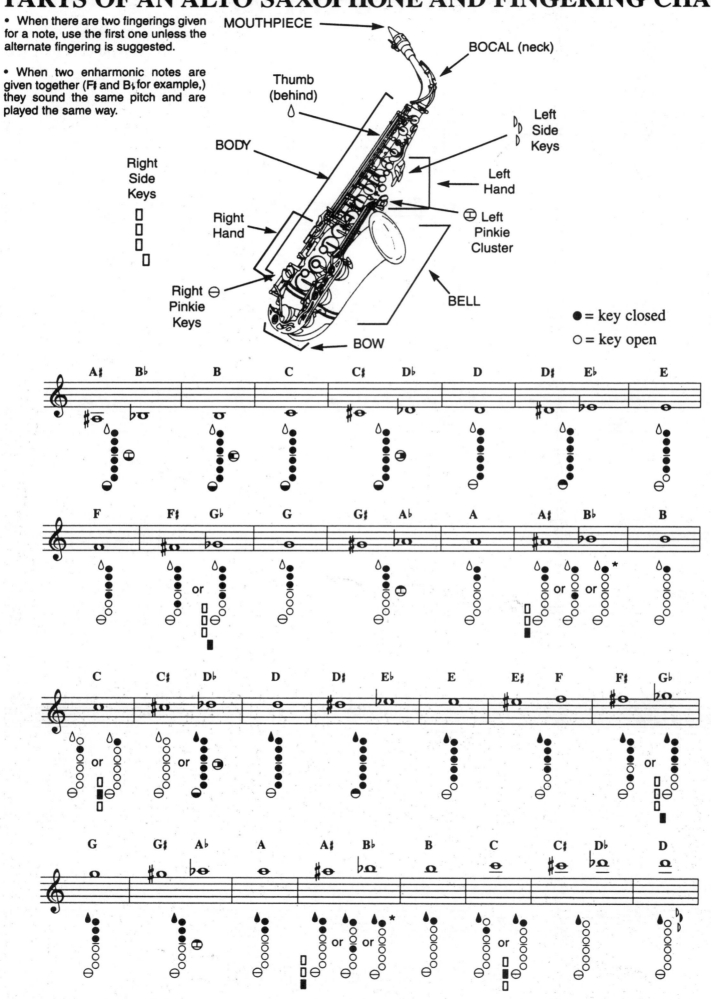

* Both pearl keys are pressed with the Left Hand 1st finger.